# ROMANS

## MOMENTOUS NEWS

10 Publishing
a division of 10 of those.com

ROMANS: Momentous News
Copyright © 2012 David Cook

First published 2002. Reprinted 2011. Reprinted 2012.

Published by 10Publishing, a division of 10ofthose.com
Unit 19 Common Bank Industrial Estate, Ackhurst Road, Chorley, PR7 1NH
Email: info@10ofthose.com
Website: www.10ofthose.com

British Library Cataloguing in Publication Data.
A catalogue record for this book is available from the British Library.

ISBN: 9781906173241

Cover Design and Typeset by Diane Bainbridge
Printed by Bell and Bain Ltd., Glasgow

# David Cook

## 50 UNDATED DEVOTIONS
## THROUGH THE BOOK OF ROMANS

# INTRODUCTION

Written by Paul in AD57 the book of Romans outlines what Christians believe, and explains the great doctrine of being made right with God – that is, 'justification by faith.'

There is no greater theme, topic or question than 'How can a person be made right with God?' This is what makes the book of Romans such a pleasure to read, study and teach. My prayer is that as you use this book to look into the Bible, it will help give you a greater grasp of God's wonderful work in bringing us, the 'unjust, unrighteous ones', to God, the 'just and righteous one', through His Son, Jesus.

**David Cook**

In these verses, Paul introduces himself, his message and his readers.

The letter begins starkly: 'Paul, servant.' A servant was without rights in the ancient world; a servant's marriage and family were not recognised; a servant's death went uninvestigated. To be a servant was a terrible thing.

However, Paul uses the title as a badge of honour, for he is Jesus Christ's slave. To be the slave of Jesus Christ was liberating.

Note that Paul's description of himself in verses 1 and 5 is a description of how he has been shaped and affirmed by the gospel.

In verses 2-4, Paul describes his message. The gospel is all about Jesus. In verse 3, Jesus' humanity is real, not imagined. In verse 4, Jesus' deity is confirmed by His bodily resurrection. The gospel is all about 'Jesus Christ our Lord'.

In verses 6-7, Paul describes his readers. Again, he describes them according to the gospel's work in them. In verse 6, they are 'called'. In verse 7, they are 'loved by God', and 'saints'.

In verse 7, Paul changes the traditional greeting 'joy and prosperity' to the more gospel-focused 'grace and peace'.

In these introductory verses note:

1. Paul describes the Scriptures (v 2), the Spirit (v 4) and God's people (v 7) as 'holy'.

2. Here, as in the rest of the New Testament, 'saints' is always in the plural. The word is derived from the word 'holy' and means 'set apart, separate'.

3. Paul forms his self-image, and the way he sees others, from the gospel. Here, according to JI Packer in *Knowing God*, is our identity: 'I am a child of God, God is my Father, heaven is my home, every day is one day nearer, my Saviour is my brother, every Christian is my brother, too.' It is an identity shaped by the gospel.

## REFLECTION

*How carefully do you form your self-image around the gospel's affirmation of you? Are you determined to see and treat others as God sees them? What difference will this make to your relationships?*

Paul planted significant churches within the Roman Empire – at Thessalonica, Corinth and Ephesus – but he did not plant the church at the centre, Rome.

He had not met the church at Rome. Yet we see his real interest in the progress of these 'brothers'. Paul gives thanks for them (v 8). He prays for them as if they were his responsibility (vv 9-10). He is a man of generous spirit. He is not given to parochial interests. If God is at work, Paul prays for and supports the work. What a model he is in ministry in contrast to other examples of professional jealousy and territorial insecurity. Paul's attitude provides a necessary corrective.

How often are our sharp criticisms of other ministries simply a thin veneer for envy?

Whether God does His work through Paul or not, Paul rejoices that God's work is being done. He gives thanks. He prays in particular that a 'way may be opened' (v 10) so that he might come to them.

Paul wants the work to continue growing and he wants to impart some spiritual emphasis (v 11) – probably the gospel – so they will be strengthened.

Paul, however, is not coming as a superior. Verse 12 makes it clear that he expects there will be mutual blessing in the visit – note the emphasis 'you and I', 'mutual' and 'each other' (v 12).

There is no aura of detached self-sufficiency about Paul. Some were alleging that he had not visited them because he was not interested. He corrects that in verse 13. His desire is for a harvest in Rome among the Gentiles because he is the apostle to the Gentiles (Acts 9:15). It is apparent that, as well as being a great theologian, Paul was a passionate missionary and evangelist.

## REFLECTION

*Reflect on Paul's generosity of spirit and his enthusiastic support of gospel work. Are you challenged by his attitude and his activities towards a people he had never met?*

*John Wesley said that parochialism has always been the enemy of the gospel. In what ways does parochialism creep into your thinking?*

Paul concludes the introduction to his letter with three 'I am' statements in verses 14, 15 and 16.

First (v 14), he says 'I am bound'. He is bound (literally, indebted) to 'Greeks and non-Greeks' – that is, to all culture – and to 'the wise and the foolish' – that is, to all classes within those cultures.

What was the source of this obligation? It came from God's grace to Paul. Once, he was the persecutor of the church. Now, he is Christ's apostle. Such grace rendered Paul a debtor to all people.

There is no sense in which grace can be earned. But receiving it so freely puts us under obligation to all. Paul probably felt more at home with people from a similar background to himself, but his sense of obligation extended to everybody without discrimination.

That is why he says (v 15) 'I am so eager'. This is a rare word in the New Testament. It means, literally, to be single-minded. Such a mind is the essence of maturity. See, for example, in Philippians 3:15 where maturity refers to the eagerness of mind expressed in the two preceding verses. Contrast that with the immaturity which Ephesians 4:14 describes as 'being tossed back and forth', as moving from one novelty to the next. FF Bruce says of Paul, 'He strikes us as a man possessed of an uncommon strength of will', such is his eagerness to preach the gospel in Rome.

Finally (v 16), he says 'I am not ashamed'. Far from being ashamed of the gospel, Paul is ready to share its message because it is the power of God to bring people to salvation. Its scope is 'everyone'. It is received by faith. Works do not earn it.

Paul longs to come to Nero's Rome as an ambassador of this gospel, with a conviction about this gospel. He will not come with a large entourage. He will not come with conventional weaponry. He will come with a message. It is a message about a crucified Jew. In Nero's Rome, this message must have seemed laughable, yet the historian, TR Glover, said that the day would come when men would call their dogs 'Nero' and their sons 'Paul'.

## REFLECTION

*How has your experience of God's grace led you to recognise your obligations? How does your sense of indebtedness show itself in your giving, your praying and your activities? Does being unashamed of the gospel lead you to share it with others?*

Most commentators agree that verses 16 and 17 constitute the theme of the letter.

Verse 17 tells us that the gospel reveals 'a righteousness from God'. Righteousness is normally used to speak of a relationship that is right. Paul may be speaking here of the righteous character of God – that God is just. When the gospel is preached, it reveals God's justice and yet, at the same time, it reveals how sinful humans can have a right relationship with Him.

Paul makes it clear that this relationship is by faith as distinct from being earned. He quotes Habakkuk 2:4, that those who are righteous are righteous simply by faith – by trusting God.

Martin Luther, the 16th century Augustinian monk, was haunted by God's righteousness and by his own sin. He tried every means the church offered in his quest for peace with God. 'I greatly longed to understand Romans and nothing stood in the way but that one expression, 'the justice of God', because I took it to mean that justice whereby God is just and deals justly in punishing the unjust. My situation was that, although an impeccable monk, I stood before God as a sinner troubled in conscience ... Then I grasped that the justice of God is that righteousness by

which, through grace and sheer mercy, God justifies us through faith. Then I felt myself to be reborn and to have gone through open doors into paradise.'

Luther went on to lecture on Romans and to write a commentary on it. It was on hearing a public reading of the introduction to Luther's commentary that John Wesley felt his heart 'strangely warmed' and was converted.

Here is a truth that has changed the course of history, a righteousness coming to us by grace, through faith, based on the finished work of Jesus Christ. This is what the gospel and 'the righteousness from God' is all about.

## REFLECTION

*What does it mean in your life each day to enjoy a right relationship with God, not because it has been earned or through merit, or even because of faith – but all because of Jesus? Why do you think seeking to win God's favour by religious activity is both impossible and unnecessary?*

Good news, bad news! Paul gives us the bad news first. (In fact, the bad news doesn't conclude until 3:21.)

God's wrath is the bad news. The reason for His wrath is people's godlessness and wickedness, as seen in their suppression of the truth (v 18). The truth is suppressed because of a determined, rebellious will. Verses 19-20 tell us that people know about God's power and deity by observation of the created order. Rather, people deliberately suppress the truth about God by exchanging the truth and glory of God for the lie of idolatry (vv 23, 25). The truth is suppressed because of a determined will.

The proper response to God is to glorify Him and to give Him thanks v 21). Instead, people worship and serve created things as though those things were the creator (v 25).

What is the nature of God's wrath? Verses 24, 26 and 28 say that God 'gave them over'. God leaves humanity to live with the fruit of its choice. This fruit comprises of general uncleanness (v 24), shameful lusts and perverse sexual activity (vv 26-27), and living contrary to God's standard (vv 28-32). Such a lifestyle becomes, therefore, the judgement of God. It is ironic that our society describes as 'gay' a lifestyle characterised by a desperate search for the fulfilment of lusts which ought

never, and will never, be satisfied.

God 'gave them over'. How different is His judgement on Ananias and Sapphira (Acts 5) which is swift and obvious, removing their hypocrisy from the church. This 'giving over' is a less obvious and more passive form of wrath. It allows sin to meander on through the life of the church and it makes life hard for God's people.

Yet mercifully, an opportunity for repentance and salvation is provided.

## REFLECTION

*How often do we get sidetracked by the symptoms rather than looking for the root cause as to why the world is the way it is?*

*According to the logic of these verses, people act the way they do (vv 24 -32) because of a theological infection: they suppress the truth of God in favour of idols (vv 18, 23, 25). The appropriate antibiotic for such an infection is theological – only the gospel provides the cure. What are the implications of this truth?*

In these verses, Paul shifts attention from the pagan idolater to the good living moralist. He shows that passing judgement on others does not exempt a person from God's wrath (vv 1-3). Passing judgement is mentioned five times.

God is generally kind, tolerant and patient. Yet, if the moralist interprets this as approval of his or her lifestyle, that attitude builds up cardiac sclerosis, a hardening of the heart (v 5). God's kindness and patience are designed to lead the unrepentant to repentance (v 4). Peter echoes this thought (2 Peter 3:9).

The Lord also makes it clear (Luke 13:1-5) that calamities remind us we are living in rebellion against God in a post-Garden of Eden environment. Calamities, too, are designed to lead us to repentance.

Thus, God speaks one message to the world: when things are good, repent; when things are disastrously bad, repent.

Repentance involves a complete change of attitude and action. It means turning away from rebelling against, or ignoring, God's claim upon us; and instead recognising that claim and, in reverence, serving Him.

This is precisely what the self-righteous moralist does not do. He or she has nothing to repent about. He or she is storing up God's wrath for the day it will be revealed (v 5). We are lost because God's justice dispenses punishment on the basis of our sinful acts.

Verses 7-11 are the most difficult verses of the letter. This is because they appear to contradict its central message: that we are justified, not by works, but through faith. But Paul does not contradict himself. Neither does he speak hypothetically.

Paul is clear that God does not have one standard for the Jew and a different one for the Gentile. God does not play favourites (v 11). Paul gives the following affirmation. Judgement is based on works, it is universal, and it is individual. There is one standard and only one. God will not be fooled by the hypocritical judgements made by self-righteous people on others. God will not be swayed by our moralising, or by our condemnation of others. God is interested in what we do (v 6) as the key to what we are.

## REFLECTION

*Where do you stand in the light of moral judgement of others? Do you think too highly of yourself? At the end of Chapter 1, did you think that you would never do the things listed there?*

Although Paul doesn't mention the legalistic Jew specifically until 2:17, he probably has such a person in mind from 2:1 as he addresses the hypocritical, self-righteous attitude of the moralist.

God does not show favouritism (v 11). When judgement comes, it will be impartial (v 6). In these verses, Paul echoes Peter's conviction at the time of Cornelius' conversion as to God's impartiality (Acts 10:34-35). Paul stresses God's impartiality in verses 9-10 with his repetition of Jew and Gentile.

So, those whose hearts are set for glory, honour and immortality (v 7) will be given eternal life, whether they are Jew or non-Jew. Similarly, those who live for self, reject truth and follow evil, will know wrath, trouble and distress (v 9).

In verses 12-16, Paul shows that God will judge people not only by their actions. They will also be accountable according to the truth they possessed. All people (Jew or non-Jew) know something of God (1:19- 20) and therefore all people have a sense of right and wrong. Such truth as people possess will provide their definition of sin. People will be judged for sin, either sin as defined by Moses' law or sin as defined by conscience. Paul shows that an inner morality is evident in the Gentiles who, without having Moses' law, often do naturally the things required by that law (vv 14-15). At judgement day (as Paul indicated in verse 16), their thoughts will accuse and excuse them when they realise it was God's law they were disobeying and obeying.

Remember, Paul is showing here how people are lost, not how they are saved. We will be judged by what we do in the light of what we know, whether it is Moses' law (as in the case of the Jew) or the law of conscience (as in the case of the Gentile). Universally, we will be found to be sinners who have acted contrary to the standard we possess.

Only the gospel, which Paul comes to in 3:21, will be able to give relief to all of us who are under the threat of God's wrath because of our sin.

## REFLECTION

*There are those who say that the pagan is better off without the gospel – let the pagan stand before God to be judged in the light of what he or she knew, for if the pagan hears and rejects the gospel, he or she will be condemned for that. Do you agree?*

*What part are you playing in seeing the gospel taken to the world? How does it affect the way you give, pray and live?*

While the Jew has not been excluded to this point, Paul now has the Jew specifically in mind.

Jews were entrusted by God with the law. Yet Paul makes it clear that mere possession of the law does not qualify one to be a guide, a light, an instructor or a teacher (vv 19-20). If the law is not lived, God is dishonoured (vv 21-23). Verse 24 is heavy in its condemnation that the Gentiles blaspheme God's character because of the lawless lives of the Jews, God's people.

Paul now turns from the law to the issue of circumcision and its inner, spiritual meaning. He argues that, just as mere possession of the law is no protection against God's condemnation, circumcision is only of value if it indicates a circumcised heart. A non-circumcised Gentile, who keeps the law and lives as though he were circumcised, will condemn the disobedient, circumcised Jew (v 27). Jewishness is not outward and physical. It is inward and spiritual. It is a circumcision of the heart (see Deuteronomy 10:16; Jeremiah 9:26; and John 8:39-45).

Thus the Jew who depends on the superiority of having God's law and the mark of the covenant in his flesh is in for a big surprise. Unless these outward signs are matched by inward experience and integrity, they are empty. (Paul illustrates this later in the case of Abraham, 4:11.)

The application to the issue of sacraments is obvious. Sacraments are empty signs if they are not matched by the inner reality they symbolise. Baptism, the initiating rite, is a symbol of our new birth, our death with Christ, and our resurrection to new life. The Lord's Supper is a reminder to us of the foundation of our right relationship with God through the work of His Son on the cross. Unless these truths are real in our experience, participation in the sacraments is of no use.

Paul's concern is to show how the Jew is lost. The Jew is lost because of disregard for God's lordship, and no amount of religious activity can compensate for that before God.

What of your heart? Is it right with God? That is the thing that counts today!

## REFLECTION

*Think about how you may be tempted to put some of your faith in doing thoroughly good things, even things like this Bible reading time. Such things can become a basis other than Christ for relationship with God.*

If, as far as God is concerned, Jews are not better off than anyone else, what advantage is there in being a Jew, one of God's people?

Paul says the advantages are many, although he lists only one (v 2). Jews have been entrusted with the very words of God, the Old Testament Scriptures. Israel's supreme privilege is that she was the first to know the mind of God.

Paul anticipates two other questions. The first is in verses 3-4. Does Jewish unfaithfulness release God from His obligation to be faithful? 'No way!' says Paul. 'God always remains faithful.' Calvin said that this is 'the primary axiom of all Christian philosophy.' God is faithfully committed to His word.

David acknowledged (v 4, see Psalm 51:4) that God was just to punish him for his sin. God is therefore faithful. He stands by His covenant promises and His covenant threats. His faithfulness is seen in His punishment of David and in His punishment of Jewish faithlessness.

The second question comes in verses 5-8. If God's faithfulness is shown when he punishes our sin, then why not continue sinning? Isn't God unjust to punish us when our sin highlights His faithfulness? 'Absolutely not!' Paul responds strongly (v 6). If that were the case, God could never judge us. Notice here how Paul accepts God's judgement as a fact. It is immovable. Your thinking is wrong if it rules out God's judgement.

Paul says that those who justify sinning because it enhances God's character are justly condemned (v 8). Paul had been slandered. It was claimed he encouraged sin, no doubt because of his emphasis on faith, not works. Others were not slandered like this, no doubt because their version of the gospel had an element of human contribution to it.

In the endeavour to justify ourselves and condemn God, we see the depth of sin in the human heart.

If a doctrine causes us to have a slack attitude to sin, and to live below God's moral standard, then it is not the truth. It is not of God.

## REFLECTION

*The condemnation of the Jews is a reminder to us that one can be zealous, knowledgeable and religious, and yet not know God. Do you know God or merely know about God?*

Following the Rabbis' pattern of substantiating their case by a list of Old Testament Scriptures, Paul quotes from Psalms, Ecclesiastes and Isaiah to summarise his argument about the state of humanity.

The repetition of 'no one', 'not even one', 'no one', 'no one', 'not even one', stands out in verses 10-12. There are no exceptions, we are all worthless. The word used is of 'milk gone off.' Having been created for a relationship with God, none of us has this relationship or displays any sign of seeking it.

This lack of relationship with God, or righteousness, is evident in our conduct. What stands out in verses 13-17 is the prominence of the 'throat', 'tongue', 'lips' and 'mouth'. The mouth is the accurate indicator of the state of the heart (Matthew 12:34).

The tongue is shown to be full of cursing, uncleanness, destruction and deceit, and our activities (vv 15-17) parallel our words. To explain the reason for this, Paul quotes from Psalm 36, 'there is no fear of God before their eyes,' the eyes being the windows for the soul.

The concluding summary of 1:18-3:20 is stated in verses 19-20. The law, God's unchangeable standard, silences all excuses. JB Phillips renders these verses

as, 'it is the straight edge of the Law that shows us how crooked we are.' The law makes us conscious of our sin. What the law will not do is provide a right standing with God through observance of its requirements.

God, therefore, justly condemns humanity, and there is no way out. We cannot work our way out. Any solution must come from God's side. We do not like to face the reality of ourselves. It is like looking at an unflattering photo. We protest about bad focus or bad developing. But here is God's perfectly focused photograph of ourselves.

It is important for us to be convicted about our hopeless state if we are to appreciate fully the wonder of the good news of salvation.

## REFLECTION

*Think about your growth in knowledge, and ask – do you know yourself? What is it that Jesus knew that kept Him from trusting people (John 2:24- 25)?*

*Reflect on Jeremiah 17:9.*

According to Leon Morris, this is perhaps the most significant paragraph ever written.

After the bleak, yet realistic, news of 1:18-3:20, we come to the momentously good news: that a right standing with God, apart from human performance, has been revealed. It comes to all who believe in the faithful work of Jesus Christ (vv 21-22).

The need for such a relationship is universal (v 23). In explaining this, Paul employs three words in common use in his time.

'Justified' (v 24). This is a legal word whereby God, the judge, declares the guilty sinner to be in the right with Him. How can God do this and remain just? He does it on the basis of the death of Jesus which has fully paid our penalty and given us acquittal.

'Redemption' (v 24). This is a word from commerce. It is what Jesus' death means to us: Jesus buys us back for God, paying the ransom price of His own perfect life.

'Sacrifice of atonement' (v 25) or 'propitiation'. This is a religious word. It explains what Jesus' death means to God. Through His death, Jesus absorbs the wrath of God due to our sin so that we don't have to take the punishment we deserve.

Thus God the Father, in the death of the Son, makes His attitude to sin patently clear (v 25). God also demonstrates His justice (v 26). His perfect Son gives His life to set us free, in that He absorbs God's just wrath against human sin. God in His love satisfies His own justice, the penalty of sin is paid, and the law is upheld. God is just and is able to be the justifier by declaring us to be in the right because of the work of Jesus.

We are not set right because of our faith. We are set right through faith (v22) and by faith (v 28). Faith links us to the work of Christ, which is the foundation of right relationship.

The foundation of this relationship is the unchanging work of Christ. God is always satisfied with the work of His Son. Hence, our relationship with God is unchanging and stable because it is based on what Jesus has done.

## REFLECTION

*In the light of the truths of this paragraph of Scripture, why is the practice of religious rituals to earn God's favour both impossible and unnecessary? Why are these truths so liberating?*

If faith is my response to what God has done, where does faith come from? If it comes from within, if it is my own contribution, then it could become a ground for my boasting.

Paul makes three points regarding justification:

1. **vv 27-28:** Justification is not earned. It is not based on keeping the law. Justification is through faith, and faith is God's gift. Otherwise justification would be a work. If it was a work, it would provide grounds for boasting. So, boasting is excluded.

2. **vv 29-30:** Justification means that God is not some localised deity having oversight and interest in the Jews alone. Justification is by faith. It is not by keeping the law or circumcision. Faith can be found in either the circumcised Jew or the uncircumcised Gentile.

3. **v 31:** In justification, God does not set aside His own justice. He does not close His eyes to broken law (see Proverbs 24:24). He does not nullify the law. Rather, our faith is directed to the work of the One who fulfilled the law's demands. The law is upheld by the provision of a perfect life offered (redemption) and God's just wrath absorbed (propitiation).

Thus, in justification, God is seen to be central. He is the source of the faith we need to link us to the work of Christ. He is the expansive God with no limited national interest. He is totally just and yet, as justifier, He is wonderfully merciful.

Augustine prayed, 'O God, demand what You will, but supply what you demand!' God demands perfection and He meets that demand in the provision of His Son.

## REFLECTION

*Do you give God the honour due to Him for the fact that you are a believer? See where faith comes from in Hebrews 12:2 and Ephesians 2:8-9. See how a person's conversion is described in John 1:12-13 and Acts 11:18, 13:48 and 16:14. How different is this to the way we describe the process of a person's conversion?*

*A former Archbishop of Canterbury, William Temple, said, 'All I have to contribute to my own salvation is the sin from which I need to be saved.'*

Paul anticipates the objection that what he is saying is so revolutionary, he simply thought it up. Objectors to the gospel today often reject it on the basis that it is just Paul's gospel.

To prove that what he is saying is not innovative, Paul gives two illustrations.

First, he takes us back to the experience of Abram. He shows that Abram was not justified by works, or he would have had something to boast about (v 2). Rather, he quotes Genesis 15:6. Abram knew the blessing of a credited righteousness by faith. This righteousness was unearned. It came as a gift to Abram through faith (vv 4-5).

Second, Paul quotes Psalm 32:1-2 to show that even the great King David anticipated the blessing of a covering for sin and that God will not count sins against the guilty. Abram has a credited righteousness; David's sins are not imputed to David himself.

So, justification is not new. The experiences of Abraham and David confirm it.

Is this justification for Jews only? This becomes Paul's next question. His response is 'No', because when Abram received the blessing (Genesis 15), he was uncircumcised. It was not until 14 years later that his circumcision took place (Genesis 17). Circumcision did not confer the blessing on Abraham. It was the sign and seal (v 11) of the blessing of a credited righteousness. So circumcision does not establish our lineage to Abraham. Ours is a spiritual lineage, faith being the common link. Abraham is the father of those who believe God and so 'walk in the footsteps of the faith that our father Abraham had' (v 12).

The law did not confer the blessing on Abraham either (vv 13-15). Righteousness was credited to him well before the law was given. The law brings only wrath because it accuses us, and we cannot keep it. Abraham's righteousness was by grace through faith, not by circumcision or by lawkeeping. Consequently, he is the father of all believers in God's promise, the gospel.

As we shall see in verses 16-25, God's method of salvation has never changed. Faith focused on God's gospel is always to be the controlling factor of our lives. Abraham is our father in this, because for him, as for us, God spoke and man believed. Here are God and man in right relationship.

## REFLECTION

*The Jews believed that having the law and being circumcised were safe shelters against God's displeasure. In what ways do we substitute things for the only safe shelter we have for salvation, namely, Jesus?*

Abraham is the father of all those who have faith. The name 'Abraham' means 'father of many nations' and that is what he is. Since Abraham is our father, he is our model or pattern. Paul says that the way God relates to Abraham is the way God relates to us.

Paul repeats (vv 16-17) that Abraham's justification was not earned but was by faith. His faith is a model for ours. Its object (v 18) was the promise of God. Faith has no inherent value apart from its object. Paul Little said, 'A strong faith in a weak bridge will not bridge the gulf, but a weak faith in a strong bridge will get you to the other side.'

Faith's strength (vv 19-20) is seen in that Abraham believed, in spite of the seeming impossibility of the promise, that the aged Sarah would bear the aged Abraham's son. The focus of his faith (v 21) was God's ability to do what He said. Abraham was not put off, because he was convinced of God's power.

The blessing that flowed (v 22) was righteousness, credited to him graciously through faith. The reason this incident was recorded was not for his sake, but for ours (vv 23-25) – that just as Abraham believed in the promise of God, so we are to believe in the work of Christ as the basis for our justification.

Just as Abraham believed God could bring an heir from one as good as dead, so we trust in the God who brought His own Son from death to life.

Verse 25 reminds us that the death of Jesus was because of our sin. His resurrection was like God's confirmation that Jesus' work on the cross had been accepted. Therefore our justification is sure.

Abraham believed the promise of redemption (v 17) and so do we (v 24). Abraham looked forward to the blessing that would come to his life (Genesis 12:3); we look back to the Redeemer who came, through whom we are blessed, as was Abraham. Abraham's life was one of great blessing. He had known persecution and harassment, yet God blessed him, and today there are approximately 1.4 billion living sons and daughters of Abraham.

He is indeed our father, our model and our pattern.

## REFLECTION

*In what way is Abraham's faith in God a challenge to our own? Which of God's promises to us are you finding hardest to trust today? Why? How does Abraham's example help you?*

Justification is such a treasure that Paul now outlines the three blessings that flow from it.

First (v 1), God is at peace with us because His justice has been satisfied. He holds nothing against us.

Second (v 1), not only do we have a relationship with an absence of anger, we have access to a gracious relationship – an unconditional, undeserved relationship without prerequisites from God's point of view.

Third (v 2), we have the certain expectation that, in the future, we will share in the glory of God (see 8:18ff). But we not only rejoice in hope, we also rejoice in suffering. Why? Because suffering leads to perseverance, which leads to character. Perseverance in the face of opposition shows the authenticity of our commitment. Such an experience leads to a freshening or new yearning for the fulfilment of our hope (v 4).

How can we be sure our hope will be fulfilled? Paul gives us three reasons:

Verse 5: God has given us the Holy Spirit who reminds us of God's love. God's love will not allow the hopes of His children to be disappointed.

Verses 6-8: The objective ground, proof, of God's love is the cross where Jesus died for our sin (vv 6, 8). Jesus' death is gracious because those for whom He died are described as sinners, helpless and enemies. This demonstration of God's love lies at the very core of Christianity, which is about the death of the innocent Son for His undeserving people.

Verses 9-11: Finally, Paul argues that our hope will not be dashed because God reconciled us when we were His enemies. Now that we are His friends, He will surely save us. Having done the greater thing, He will do the comparatively lesser, the fulfilment of our hope.

Therefore we can be sure that our hope of glorification will not be dashed.

## REFLECTION

*God says having two witnesses in a case is important (see Deuteronomy 19:15). Who are the two witnesses to God's love mentioned here? How are they different? What should the blessings of justification cause you to do?*

# DAY 16

Martyn Lloyd-Jones calls this section the core of the letter. Here Paul sums up all that he has said about how God has released us from the penalty for sin. He shows that there were only ever two 'camps', two representatives – Adam (v 14), and his counter part, Jesus Christ (v 15). We are represented either by the first Adam or the second Adam.

The first man, Adam, by an act of disobedience, brought condemnation and death to us all (vv 16-17). The second Adam, however, brings grace and the gift of righteousness to His people (v 17).

Paul also shows (vv 18-19) that the way we are justified parallels the way we were condemned. Adam trespassed and we were all condemned (v 18). Christ obeyed and we were all justified (v 18). The act of the one renders the 'many' either condemned or justified.

How were we condemned? God imputed to us the disobedience of our representative head, Adam. Before we had actually sinned, Adam's sin was debited to our account. That is why people were condemned before sin was defined by Moses and the law (vv 12-14). They were condemned because Adam's sin was imputed to them.

The way we are condemned is, in the case of Christ and the believer, a pattern for our justification. All the righteousness and obedience of Christ was imputed to us. It was credited to our account and we were declared righteous (v 19).

What then happened to all our debits – Adam's trespass and our personal sin? It was reckoned to Christ's account. He did not become actually sinful any more than we became actually perfect; but, as with a bookkeeping entry, our sin was debited to him. He died to pay its penalty, and now His righteousness is credited to us (see 2 Corinthians 5:21).

When God looks at our account now, He sees only the accounted perfection of Jesus. Law defined sin and made it obvious, but God's grace in the work of Christ is always sufficient to cover human sin and bring us, through credited righteousness, to eternal life (vv 20-21).

It is through faith that we transfer from the camp of Adam (the camp of our birth) to the camp of Christ (the camp, according to John, of the children of God). The first camp is by birth, and the second by rebirth (John 1:12-13).

## REFLECTION

*Again we are reminded (4:3 and 5:18) how God acts consistently in the Old and New Testaments. The Bible is thus one book of the one God. How does this affect your view of yourself as a believer, and of the Bible as your book?*

Paul anticipates the big question: Since grace increases to cover sin (5:20), why not sin more so that God's grace increases even more? If God sees us perfect because of the work of Jesus, why worry about sin?

Paul responds to any thinking that encourages a slack attitude to sin with 'By no means!' (v 2). He goes on to tell us why we are to be holy.

We are to be holy because we died with Christ. His death was a proxy death for us. We were with Him on the cross, with Him in the tomb, and with Him in His resurrection (vv 3-4). When Christ died for sin, we died to sin. Baptism, Paul says, is a constant reminder of our participation in Christ's death and resurrection. Union with Jesus is the key to our justification and holiness.

When we died with Christ, we died to sin. Sin did not die; rather our physical body, which sin used as its instrument, was taken out of gear (v 6). Conversely, we have been raised with Christ to a new life (vv 4, 5, 8). This new life is never ending (v 9). Qualitatively, it is a life lived in knowledge of God and in reverence for Him (v 10).

Significantly, to this point in the letter, Paul has not given one command. When it comes to justification, we have no contribution to make, so nothing can

be commanded of us. But in verses 11-14, he gives a number of orders.

The first (v 11), is attitudinal. We are to make the same calculation about ourselves as God has made about us; that is, that we are dead to sin and alive to God. As God sees us, so we are to see ourselves. Then (v 12), we do not let sin reign over us. Next (v 13), we do not keep going to sin's temple to make offerings there. Rather (v 13), we commit ourselves once and for all to God's lordship.

The reason for this is that we live in a relationship not ruled by observing law, or by earning merit. We live in an unconditional, undeserved relationship of grace.

The key to holiness is to recognise our solidarity with Christ and to stop sinning. As we resist temptation, God will help us to resist it (see Philippians 2:12-13).

## REFLECTION

*What does it mean for you to have eternal life (6:10)? See John 17:3. How does this section help you resist temptation?*

Paul is still talking about holiness. Today, he takes us to the slave market. A person can claim to be anyone's slave, but the reality is that the master they obey enslaves them.

Paul pursues the question of those who are justified and their attitude to sin. There are only two possible masters (v 16) – sin ('Master Sin') or obedience and righteousness ('Master Righteousness'). The essence of sin, therefore, is disobedience.

Paul further identifies and describes these two 'Masters' in verse 19. 'Master Sin' pays a wage: it is earned, it is deserved (vv 21, 23), it is death. Death is separation from God. However, slavery to obedience ('Master Righteousness') brings about a benefit or gift. That benefit is eternal life, life in relationship with God. Since we were born to the slavery of 'Master Sin', how did we come to obedience? The answer comes in verse 17. Paul gives thanks to God that 'you wholeheartedly obeyed the form of teaching to which you were entrusted'. In other words, they placed their confidence in the gospel. Notice that the gospel was not entrusted to them; they were entrusted to it.

Through the obedience of the gospel that comes from faith (1:5), we come under the shelter and security of the gospel, which now keeps us safe. So why go back to the former master, Sin? We owe him nothing. He pays us death and we are ashamed of what we did with him (v 21).

This is the second image regarding holiness: first, union with Christ in death and resurrection; second, set free from 'Master Sin' and enslaved to 'Master Righteousness' (v 18).

Verse 23 provides the summary: sin pays a wage (death), God gives a gift (eternal life). The gift comes to us because of the work of Christ Jesus our Lord. We cannot have life apart from Him.

## REFLECTION

*Sinless perfection is not a reality for life on earth (see 1 John 1:5-10). But do you take seriously enough your responsibility to resist temptation?*

Paul has used the image of our solidarity with Jesus (6:1-14) – we died, we were buried and we were raised with Him. He has used the image of the master/slave relationship (6:15-23). Finally, now, he uses the image of death (7:1-6).

The point Paul makes is that death frees a person from the binding of the law (v 3). If a woman's husband dies, she is free to remarry. But if she marries while her husband is still alive, she becomes an adulteress. The difference is that death legitimately terminates marriage.

By dying to the law, the believer is legitimately free to 'marry' (that is, to be united with) Christ and thus to serve in the new way of the Spirit (vv 4-6).

What then is our relationship to the law? Do we fear it like the legalist does? Do we hate it like the person who sees the law as the source of our problems? No. We love the law. We do so because it represents the will of God and because Christ kept it. The law is holy and good (v 13), though it will not save us. The problem is not the law but our sin (vv 8-9, 11). The law's role is to identify sin (vv 7-8) and to show us our condemnation as sinners (vv 9-11).

When was Paul alive apart from law (v 9)? It was probably when he believed he had lived consistently with the law (see Philippians 3:6). When he realised the true jurisdiction of the law, not only over outward actions but inner attitudes, he realised how lost he was.

So Paul summarises (v 13): the good law identified sin and condemned Paul as a sinner. In that way, it prepared him for the Saviour to come (7:24-25).

The law gets us ready for the coming of Christ as it brings conviction of sin (see Galatians 3:24-25). As law-abiding believers, we love the law yet we recognise its limitation. It cannot save or sanctify us. The problem lies with us. To blame the law, according to FF Bruce, is like the prisoner in gaol blaming the law which put him there as though it were the law's fault and not his own.

## REFLECTION

*Do you seek to honour the law as did our Lord, Jesus Christ? How often do you search your life in the light of the law, so as to realise the extent of your sinfulness? It is only in the light of conviction of our sinfulness that we realise the greatness of the rescue we have in Jesus.*

There are three options for understanding who is described as the 'I' in these verses, and of the state he is in.

**OPTION 1:** Is Paul speaking of himself as a believer? If he is, he is describing normal Christian experience.

**OPTION 2:** Is Paul speaking of himself as an 'unspiritual' believer? If so, it would introduce an unbiblical third category of person. In addition to the non-Christian and the Christian, there would now be the 'semi-Christian'.

**OPTION 3:** Is Paul describing his experience with the law, as a God-fearing Israelite? In this case, the experience he describes, best summarised in verse 19 as 'I don't do the good I want to do, the evil I don't want to do is what I do', is the typical experience of every Israelite who seeks to keep God's law as the way to righteousness.

As to these options, look at Romans 9:30-33 and 10:3 to see that the Israelites sought to establish their own righteousness through law keeping. Paul explains in today's verses and elsewhere that this is an impossible quest. 'What a wretched man I am! Who will rescue me from this body of death?' in verse 24 is the typical cry of the one under law who cannot keep it. Paul sees himself as bound to his body of death, a reference to King Mezentius who tied living criminals to the decomposing corpses of their victims. The law is good (7:12) but it is powerless to change us or to enable us to keep it.

The cry of triumph in verse 25 follows closely on the cry of anguish in verse 24. Chapter 8 fully describes the deliverance we have in Christ, climaxing with our glorification (vv 18ff).

According to the first option, verse 19 is an accurate description of the believer's experience with good and evil. But, if this is typical of us, how can the exhortation of 6:19 not to offer our bodies in slavery to wickedness but rather to righteousness be meaningful, since the normal experience is one of frequent defeat? Also, how can 7:19 and 8:9-11 both be accurate pictures of the believer when they seem to say contrary things about the one person? Surely they cannot both be an accurate description of a Christian.

The first option does not seem to fit the context of Paul's argument as well as the third one does. Our performance will not be perfect this side of glory, but the desperate defeat and wretchedness described in these verses is evidence of the law's impotence to save and of the great need of unsaved Israel to come to Christ where there is no condemnation (8:1).

## REFLECTION

*Think about the dilemma of the God-fearer who has God's law, who desires to be obedient and yet does not know Christ. Thank God for the deliverance we have through Christ from the condemnation we deserve.*

We come to an especially majestic section of the letter. In it, Paul shows two things.

First, we are delivered from the just condemnation of the law. The law could not justify us because we could not keep it (v 3), so God provided His Son who perfectly met the requirements of the law (v 4) and then took our place as the perfect offering for sin (v 3).

Second, while the sinful nature of the 'old man' remains a powerful force within the believer, God has given the believer a powerful gift, the indwelling Spirit who enables us to do God's will. (There are more references to the Spirit in Chapter 8 than in all the other chapters of the letter.)

In verses 5-8, Paul contrasts life in the Spirit with life in the flesh.

Being children of God means that we have the Holy Spirit (v 9). (See Acts 2:38 for the great blessings of the new covenant.)

The Spirit revitalises our ageing, dying bodies (vv 10-11).

The Spirit leads us to put to death the misdeeds of the body (vv 14-15). He empowers us for godly living.

The Spirit gives us deep assurance that we are God's children (vv 15-16). We can relate to God on the most intimate basis and call Him 'Abba Father'.

The very essence of being a child is that we have a parent. Since we have a parent, we are heirs and have an inheritance (v 17). Here we are reminded that we are heirs of God our Father and will share the inheritance with God the Son, our elder brother (v 29b). However, this inheritance will not be split 50/50. Being a 'coheir' means that everything that is Christ's is ours, so it is 100/100. Our entry to our inheritance is like His. For Him the inheritance was the crown via the cross; for us too it will be glory via present suffering (v 17).

Here Paul answers two questions: Am I condemned by my past life? Does God leave me without resources in the battle with the flesh? The answer to both is 'No.' Because of what Jesus has done, we are not condemned, and because God has given us His Holy Spirit, we are not without resources.

## REFLECTION

*How do you encourage the hope of our inheritance to be more dominant in your thinking? The Puritans thought about heaven on a daily basis. Why?*

*(See 1 Thessalonians 1:3.) Do you?*

 **DAY 22**

As children of God, we are waiting for our promised inheritance (v 17). What is our present experience as we wait?

First, Paul says it is one of suffering (v 18). In verse 35, he outlines what he has in mind. He tells us that not only do we groan under the weight of present suffering (v 23), but the whole of creation groans under the frustration of its generation-growth-decay cycle. The creation is waiting for its liberation from the bondage of this cycle, and that will happen when the sons of God are revealed, that is, when Christ returns (v 19).

We have received the down payment of our salvation in the person of the Holy Spirit (v 23). We groan as we wait for the rest of the payment, when our bodies will be transformed (1 Corinthians 15:35ff).

Our present experience is one of suffering and groaning. Paul says there should be none of the unreal positivism that dominates those churches which claim the experience of life is one triumph after another. Note also, there is none of the constant gloom that may suit some personalities, for we are not as we were before we were believers. We have received the Holy Spirit, the down payment, the first fruits which guarantee the rest is to come (v 23).

Secondly, Paul says our experience involves weakness (v 26). This is not a moral weakness, but the weakness of ignorance. Sometimes life is so complex we simply do not know the appropriate things to pray for. However, the down payment, the Spirit, does know. He intercedes effectively for us in a way that is consistent with God's will when we may not know what God's will is in the situation (v 27).

So here is our present experience, realistic, yet not one of unrelieved gloom; for through the work of Jesus, God has given us His Holy Spirit. The Spirit strengthens us to be holy (v 13). He revitalises us (v 11). He reminds us that we are God's children (v 16) and that we are on intimate terms with God (v 15). He is the first fruits (v 23), the guarantee of full salvation to come. He is the informed intercessor who prays for us (vv 26-27).

## REFLECTION

*How well do you know the ministry of the Holy Spirit in your experience? Do you recognise His work as outlined above? Do you thank God that the Holy Spirit has been given to you because of the work of Jesus? Note, again, the two great blessings of salvation in Acts 2:38.*

Suffering, groaning and a sense of our own ignorance surround us. Is there any order to the seeming chaos of life?

Paul answers 'Yes' in verse 28. God is at work in all things for our good. However, Paul limits this principle in two ways.

The first limitation is by reference to the identity of those for whom God works, described as those who love God, who have been called by God. This is not some universal principle that things just have a way of turning out well. No, God works in all things to turn them to the good of His own people.

Paul limits the principle, secondly, by defining (in v 29) the good for which God works. He takes us to eternity past to show that in God's foreknowledge, before we existed, God knew us as His own. His knowledge initiated the relationship. It is not as though God knew we would choose Him and then fitted in with our choice. To those who were thus known, God gave a destiny that they should be like Jesus (v 29). Becoming like Jesus is the good for which God works. It is not our health and comfort and wealth, but our godliness which he promises to achieve.

In other words, God's purpose is to build a family like Jesus. Jesus is the firstborn, the one in unique relationship with the Father, but He is also one of us because He is the firstborn brother.

Is our conformity to the image of our elder brother guaranteed? How do we know the glory referred to in 8:17, 19, 21 and 23 will be ours? Paul says in verse 30 that it is as sure as the eternal purposes of God; for just as God has predestined us, called us and justified us, so He will glorify us. Paul places glorification, a future experience, in the past tense to underline its certainty. As God has completed the first three, so He will complete the last, our glorification.

These are such comforting truths. We are spiritual rulers; there is nothing we will meet today that we do not reign over. Nothing can come our way that is not ultimately good for the health of our soul. God will be at work in everything we meet today so that it is for our good, making us like Jesus.

This is most comforting news for us, and most frustrating for our enemies.

## REFLECTION

*Do you trust the God of the sovereign hidden hand and look for His hand in all things?*

Spurgeon said the doctrine of election is the most 'stripping doctrine of all.' It is humbling. It means that our salvation began with God. This is the plain teaching of the Bible, yet we don't like to be humbled so we reject talk of election.

Wherever the New Testament talks about election, it is always in the context of the great blessings we have.

Election is a reminder that we should not get big-headed about these blessings. It is not because of us but because of Him that we are His and enjoy such blessings.

Paul concludes this first section of Romans by asking and answering four questions about our security:

1. **Verse 31:** Is there any enemy who can effectively defeat us? No, since God is for us! In giving His own Son, God has shown the extent of His support.

2. **Verse 33:** Is there any barrister who can effectively make a charge stick against us? No, God has irrevocably declared us to be in the right with Him!

3. **Verse 34:** Is there any accuser who can effectively condemn us? No, Jesus who is constantly at God's right hand will always silence any accusation!

4. **Verse 35:** Is there anyone or any situation that can effectively separate us from God's love? No, he lists all the possibilities: no person in the created order, no situation, no extremity – nothing can separate us from the blessings of our salvation in Christ and from God's loving oversight in all these things. Paul concludes (v 37) that we are super conquerors because of God who loved us.

Paul pushes language to its extreme here. At this point, one feels sorry for his note-taker, Tertius (16:22)!

What a magnificent conclusion to the first part of the book. JI Packer identified his favourite chapter in the Bible as that which begins with 'There is no condemnation' and ends with 'nothing can separate us from the love of God.'

No condemnation. No separation. That is momentous news.

## REFLECTION

*Think about your eternal security. How safe are you? (See John 10:27 -30.) Should such security cause you to be careless? (See Hebrews 3:12 -15, 4:6-7 and 6:4-6.)*

These chapters represent the trough and peak of human experience. Humanity disobeyed God's clear instruction (Genesis 2:16-17) and as a result separation and friction entered into our experience.

Adam and Eve sensed a separation between each other; their sense of openness was lost (3:7). The man blamed God and the woman (3:12) blamed the snake.

The man and woman hid from God; their glad fellowship was gone (3:10).

Their environment was going to be against them: Adam would have to deal with weeds (3:18), and Eve would have to handle pain in giving birth (3:16).

They would both find friction in their relationship; she would seek to assert herself over him, and he would seek to despotically rule her (3:16).

They would both face the inevitability of death (3:19), which is part of God's curse upon them. They said to God, 'We want paradise, we don't want you', and God expelled them from paradise (3:23-24). Ever since, we have all lived in a post-Eden environment.

The trough of friction, separation and condemnation is matched by the peak of no condemnation, no separation, of Romans 8.

In Romans 8, we find substantial restoration and fellowship with God, but we still face an antagonistic environment that causes us to groan (8:22-23) as we await the return to the Eden paradise we lost because of sin. We have received the down payment (here and now, in the person of the Holy Spirit), on all we will receive, there and then (8:23).

Why can this restoration occur? It is all because of the work of Jesus described in three words in Romans 3:24-25: 'justified', 'redeemed' and 'sacrifice of atonement'.

Paul never lets us forget that we are not self-made people. We know substantial restoration and have the hope of heaven because of the work of Jesus. These blessings cannot be had apart from that work. They are for believers only; they are only for the children of Abraham.

## REFLECTION

*Note in these verses how Paul underlines that what we have, we have because of Jesus: Romans 3:22, 26; 4:24-25; 5:1, 9, 11, 21; 6:23; 7:24-25; 8:1, 34, 39. What are the implications of this for your faith?*

Paul's elated confidence at the end of chapter 8 now turns to 'great sorrow and unceasing anguish' (v2) as he thinks about Israel's obstinate resistance of the gospel. Does this represent a failure of God's faithfulness to keep his promises to save Israel, or a failure of his word (v6)? The answer is no: God always intended to save a remnant of Israel. Even among Abraham's children he chose Isaac, not Ishmael; and Jacob, not Esau (v7-13).

Does this election mean that God is unjust (v14)? No, says Paul. It is not a justice issue—all people deserve condemnation. God is sovereign in the exercise of his mercy, and in the exercise of whom he hardens, such as Pharaoh (v15-18).

If that is the case, then why does God still hold us responsible if human unbelief is a result of God's hardening of the human heart (v19)? Such an argument is the equivalent of clay complaining to the potter about the use to which it is put. The potter makes different vessels out of the same lump of clay (v20-21).

Why does God act like this? Why doesn't he just elect everyone? He did this to glorify himself (v22-24): the unbeliever, by his stubborn resistance, elevates God's patience; the believer, by his undeserved acceptance, elevates God's mercy.

Paul then quotes Hosea and Isaiah (v25-29) to show that it was always God's intention to save a remnant of both Jews and non-Jews.

Those who love the Bible but have a problem accepting the doctrine of election will have an obvious problem here. It is an affront to our pride to be told that we make no contribution to our own salvation; salvation is based solely on the electing mercy of God, and that is undeserved.

Spurgeon said this is the 'most comforting doctrine of all'. Rejection of this truth robs God of the sole glory due to him for our salvation, and also robs the believer of the 'sweet, pleasant and unspeakable comfort'[1] that comes from knowing our salvation is God's decision and he will never change his mind.

Here is the antidote to every vestige of self-righteousness: there is nothing here for us to feel superior about, for God chose us despite ourselves, not because of anything we have done. Here is the great motivation for prayer and evangelism: God has an elect people, but we don't know who they are (Acts 18:10). We must take the gospel out in the assurance that God knows who they are, and he will call them to faith when they hear the gospel.

## REFLECTION

*Why should God's unconditional choice of the church surprise us, since he chose Israel unconditionally? Do you think we have a problem with the teaching of Romans 9 because it is hard to understand, or because it is hard to accept?*

Two images are used here of Jesus. The first is that of 'a stumbling-stone' (9:33) and the second is as 'the end of the law' (10:4).

Israel stumbled over Jesus. Rather than finding refuge in him, because they did not recognise that the law was pointing forward to him, Israel instead treated the law as the means of their salvation.

Paul's anguish for Israel is a result of their choosing the wrong path. They chose to pursue righteousness by obeying the law (9:31; 10:3) and, therefore, did not submit to God's way of setting people right with himself.

Verse 2 tells us that although Israel is sincere and zealous (the qualities necessary for correctness in this postmodern world), she is wrong; for despite her zeal, Israel is ignorant (v3). Paul sets out the two possible routes to righteousness in verses 5-7. In verse 5, righteousness is by keeping the law, and in verses 6-7, by contrast, righteousness is not by human achievement but by God's provision. Christ does not need to be brought down (v6) - he 'came down' in the incarnation. He does not need to be brought up (v7) - he 'came up' in the resurrection; both of these are God's provision. So is God's gift of righteousness, which is not a result of human achievement.

All religions in one way or another can be categorised as achievement-based. Biblical Christianity alone can be categorised as provision-based. Righteousness is something God requires, and provides - to all those who have faith in his Son. Having faith in Jesus means

having a particular conviction about Jesus: that God has raised him from the dead (v9). What the heart believes, the mouth confesses: that he is indeed Lord, and God in the flesh (designated as such by his resurrection from the dead, cf. 1:4).

In verse 11, Paul quotes Isaiah, saying that anyone who has this conviction and confession of Jesus will never be shamed, and that God has only this one way of putting people right with himself. In verses 12 and 13, he says it is the same for everyone, Jews or Gentiles. Everyone who calls on the name of Jesus as God, because of his resurrection, will be saved.

This is indeed momentous news. Think of all those who labour under the burden of 'religion' - law-keeping. Whether it is Christian 'religion' or not, it is equally tragic. It is both an impossible task, to achieve God's righteousness; and it is totally unnecessary, because Christ, our substitute, has met God's righteous requirements on our behalf. 'Religion' is doubly tragic - both impossible and unnecessary.

## REFLECTION

*Why is provision, rather than achievement, such good news? Augustine prayed, 'O God, demand what you will, but supply what you demand'. What does God demand? How does he supply this demand?*

Since faith in Jesus is the way of righteousness, and since God is sovereign in the choosing of his elect, how does God call his elect to himself? Paul's reasoning is very structured at this point. Notice what he says:

Those who *call* on the name of the Lord will be saved. (v13)

- **How can they call without *belief*? (v14)**
- **How can they believe without *hearing*? (v14)**
- **How can they hear without *preaching*? (v14)**
- **How can they preach unless they are *sent*? (v16)**

Even the feet of those who preach such a momentous message are beautiful.

Not all who hear the message necessarily believe; not all will be saved; but God is actively calling out his people through the hearing of the gospel (v16-17).

The Heidelberg Catechism, question 65, asks: 'It is by faith alone that we share in Christ and all his blessings: where then does that faith come from?' Answer 65 responds: 'The Holy Spirit produces it in our hearts through the preaching of the holy gospel ...'

Didn't Israel hear (v18)? Certainly they did: the apostles took very seriously their responsibility of taking the gospel first to the Jews.

Didn't they understand (v19-21)? They understood grace well enough to make them jealous of others' reception

of it (v19). God is sovereign in this process (v20) but Israel is personally responsible for her disobedience and obstinacy (v21).

The doctrine of election is often attacked because, it is said, it renders the believer paralysed at the point of evangelism. Not so, says Paul (v1, 17). This doctrine provides the greatest motivation for evangelism. We are not to be put off by people's resistance: our confidence in evangelism does not rest on our ability to explain or people's ability to understand, but rests on God's mercy. That is why prayer must accompany the clear, widespread presentation of the gospel, so that the sovereign God will do his work of calling out his people as the gospel is explained.

Is the preaching spoken of in verse 15 a particular calling? Strictly speaking, no; but the preacher needs to know that he is sent, and commissioned by God. (See Matthew 9:38 for a similar emphasis.)

## REFLECTION

*What is the logic behind each of the steps Paul mentions in verses 11-15? How do these truths challenge your commitment to supporting the widespread preaching of the gospel? How can you encourage preachers and evangelists today?*

Paul himself, a Jew, is an example of the fact that God has not abandoned Israel (v1). God has always reserved a remnant who will never be abandoned: Paul, Elijah and the 7,000 (see 1 Kings 19:10, 14, 18) are examples of that (v4). So too at the present time, Paul says, there is a small 'remnant' within Israel (v6). This remnant is chosen by grace, not by merit (v5-6).

Israel's resistance and blindness is no surprise to God. In fact he gave them this spirit, this insensitivity to revelation: this is his judgement upon their refusal to heed the gospel (v8). The darkening of their spiritual eyes (v9-10) has overtaken them all, except for the faithful remnant.

Paul shows, by quoting Deuteronomy 29 and Psalm 69 (in v8-10), that this is the verdict of Scripture, that God superintends all this activity. But what is his purpose in all this? Is this hardening permanent? No (v11). Charles Hodge says, 'The rejection of the Jews is not total, neither is it final'[2].

In the book of Acts we see this pattern repeatedly: the gospel comes to the Jew first, then upon their rejection it goes to the Gentiles, who accept it: and thus Israel becomes envious of the Gentiles' blessing (v11). Paul therefore makes much of his ministry to the Gentiles, for this is a means of arousing Israel to envy and bringing her to her senses

(v13-14). In the economy of God, Israel's stumbling is the means of so many Gentiles coming to Christ.

In verse 16 Paul uses two metaphors: dough in baking, and the root and branch of a tree. The principle is that if one part is holy, then the whole of the bake run or the whole tree is holy. Therefore, if the first fruit or root is the Lord's then the rest is his as well; if the Patriarchs are God's then those who follow them, elect Israel and elect Gentiles, are his as well; if Paul and his fellow Jewish believers are the Lord's then all who follow them with faith in Christ are the Lord's as well.

These are difficult verses. However, we can see that God has a plan and he is working it out. He is the great super-intending evangelist, working to the salvation indicated in verse 26. Trusting him does not lead us to inactivity, but rather, to the activity indicated in Romans 1:14-16.

## REFLECTION

*What do you think about God's ongoing purpose for the Jews? Should we be especially supportive of evangelism among Jews? Why / why not?*

The gospel always quells human pride and arrogance. God is attracted by our weakness and repelled by our pride. Gentiles should not be proud, for just as God did not spare unbelieving Israel, so too he will not spare unbelief in those branches that have been ingrafted (v17-21) – that is, in the Gentiles.

God is both kind and stern, and if he grafts a wild branch, like the Gentiles, into the tree then he is more than able to regraft the natural branches (Israel) when they believe in Christ (v22-24).

The mystery (referred to in Ephesians 1:9-10 and 1 Thessalonians 4:13ff) is now revealed: God is at work through hardening and softening, to bring the full number of Gentiles into his kingdom, so that 'all Israel' (that is, all the elect Jews and Gentiles) will be saved. Therefore, the hardening of ethnic Israel is both temporary and purposeful.

This means there is a place in God's purposes for ongoing evangelism among both Jews and Gentiles.

Jewish resistance → Gentile belief → Jewish envy → the Gentile number complete → and in this way all Israel are saved. (All Israel consists of believing Jews and believing Gentiles.)

This may mean that in the end times (v15) we might well see widespread turning of Jews to Jesus as the Christ.

Their estrangement has been the means of Gentiles coming to faith (v28) and all God's promises to them will yet be fulfilled. God's purpose is to be merciful to Jew and Gentile alike (v30-32).

Verses 33-36 are a final doxology that closes chapters 1-11. God's wisdom and knowledge is beyond ours and is not a result of our advice - he is in no way indebted to us. God is the originator of all things - 'from him'; the director of all things - 'through him'; and the object of all things - 'to him'. He is to be praised. Amen.

'The leading principle is that God is the source of all good; that in fallen people there is neither merit nor ability; that salvation consequently is all of grace, as are sanctification, pardon, election and glory.'[3] For from him and through him and to him are all things - and so to him be glory forever and ever. Amen!

## REFLECTION

*Reflect on God's merciful dealings with you. What is mercy? How has God shown you mercy? In what ways does this passage encourage you to humility?*

Paul uses the word 'therefore' on three occasions in his letter to the Romans, to signal a pause in his argument and to begin to apply his teaching to the lives of his readers.

Having established that righteousness is both God's requirement and God's provision (3:21-26) and that this is nothing new, as demonstrated in the experience of Abraham (chapter 4), he comes to his first conclusion in 5:1: 'Therefore, since we have been justified through faith...'

Righteousness as God's provision through faith has three benefits:

- We know that God is at peace with us because of what Christ has done (5:1);

- We have access, by faith, into an undeserved and unconditional relationship with God, in which we now stand (5:2a);

- We have an assured future: the glory of God (5:2b).

Paul goes on to show how God's love proves the certainty of that future: his love is seen in the gift of the Holy Spirit (5:5) and the gift of his Son (5:6-8). Righteousness that is provided by God shows itself in our life in a concern for practical holiness. It is union with Jesus which brings about justification and which produces sanctification, the necessary fruit of that new life (6:14).

The battle against the old sinful nature, outlined in chapter 7, leaves Paul with two questions: will he be condemned by his own lack of holiness? And does God leave us under-resourced in this battle against the sinful nature? The first of these is answered by the next 'therefore' in 8:1: 'Therefore, there is now no condemnation for those who are in Christ Jesus...'

Our poor performance will not condemn us because of what Christ has done. The old covenant law of Moses condemned us because none of us could keep it (v3), but God sent his son to fulfil the righteous requirement of the Law and to become a sin offering in our place (v3-4). 'No condemnation now I dread', not because of our record, but because of Jesus' work on our behalf.

Paul outlines God's purpose to preserve a remnant people for himself made up of both Jews and non-Jews. This remnant belongs to God because of the sovereign exercise of his mercy (9:14-15; 11:25-27). In response to these mercies of God, Paul comes to his last 'therefore': 'Therefore, I urge you brothers, in view of God's mercy, to offer your bodies as living sacrifices...' This, he says, is the fitting response to what God has done in adding us to his remnant people.

## REFLECTION

*How often do you take time to reflect about God's mercy in your life and your own response to it? What are the blessings of God's mercies in which you rejoice today?*

The biggest problem faced by the believer in his thinking is to keep on recognising that God's mercy is not a human achievement. It is so natural, given the conditional nature of human love and acceptance, to think that God's love and acceptance, likewise, is conditional. We need to keep correcting our thinking to see that we are not working to achieve and maintain God's mercy, but rather, all we do is a response to God's mercy.

Mercy is always a precondition, and it is never a human achievement. Mercy is the environment from which Paul's urging springs in verse 1.

He comes to his third great 'therefore' in Romans - see 5:1; 8:1; and now 12:1. In view of God's merciful dealings with us, here is the 'spiritual' or more literally, the 'appropriate' or 'reasonable' response. Here then is the very heart of appropriate living: to 'offer our bodies as living sacrifices'. Just as the old covenant believer would bring a dead animal sacrifice in order to maintain relationship with God, we are to come as living sacrifices, as a reasonable response to the unconditional relationship we have with God and which he has established.

All the Old Testament sacrifices anticipate the final, central sacrifice of Jesus on the cross. His death makes the Old Testament sacrificial system redundant. It is now as superseded as old currency when a new currency system is introduced. However, his death makes the other New Testament sacrifice, the sacrifice of yourself, totally reasonable.

This reasonable response, Paul says, is both wholehearted (holy) and pleasing to God. When Eric Liddell, of Chariots of Fire fame, was asked why he kept running, he responded, 'When I run I feel His pleasure'.

There are things which God takes no pleasure in, like sin and the death of the wicked; but you can know God's pleasure today as you live fittingly and offer your body to him as a living sacrifice. In 2 Corinthians 5:14-15 Paul tells us what went through the mind of Jesus when he was dying on the cross. He says, 'and he died for all, that those who live should no longer live for themselves but for him who died for them and was raised again'. Recognising Christ's purpose and living consistently with it is eminently reasonable.

Isaac Watts puts it like this:
*Love so amazing, so divine,*
*Demands my soul, my life, my all.*

The missionary C.T. Studd put it like this: 'If Jesus Christ be God, and died for me, then no sacrifice can be too great for me to make for him.'

## REFLECTION

*Think about how Paul passionately urges, but note that his appeal is to our reason. Why do you think God is pleased with you as a living sacrifice? Are you living reasonably, according to these verses, or foolishly according to the world's dictates?*

Paul describes in verse 2 what it means to be a living sacrifice. First, there is a 'don't': 'do not conform any longer to the pattern of this world'; 'don't let the world squeeze you into its mould' (J.B. Phillips). The world judges the reasonable response of verse 1 as foolishness. The world judges being a living sacrifice as fanatical, and Paul says we must not share the world's assessment. Rather, do be transformed by the renewal of your mind.

In verse 1 we are told of the reasonable response. Now in verse 2 we are told that transformation comes via renewal of the mind. The world's view of the self is that self is good: it is to be nurtured, polished, bragged about, asserted. Paul makes it clear in Romans that we are to assert about ourselves what the gospel asserts about us. See his self-description in 1:1 and how he describes the believers in 1:6-7.

The first command in Romans comes in 6:11 and has to do with the mind: '... count yourselves dead to sin but alive to God in Christ Jesus'. Here, 'count yourselves' is the verbal form of the 'reasonable response' of 12:1. Paul's line of thinking looks like this:

Renew the mind → Think about yourself the way God does → Transformed lifestyles as a result → Your body as a living sacrifice to God.

In Romans 1:21 and 28 Paul says that a fruit of humanity's lack of relationship with God is futile thinking and minds which are depraved or scrambled, unable to make proper moral judgements. That is the typical characteristic of the mind of the natural person. But in Romans 12:2 we see the reversal of that: the believer has a renewed mind and that mind recognises and approves God's good, pleasing, and perfect will.

Christians are human beings who are human 'becomings' in the process of change - on the way to perfection, our eternal state. This change comes via the renewal of the mind and in response to the mercies of God.

Today you go to work reasonably as a living sacrifice to God, or unreasonably as your own person, to do your own thing by and for yourself.

The world says that, 'living sacrifices' are fundamentalist freaks. You know that being a 'living sacrifice' is the only reasonable way to live for one who is dead to sin, but alive to God in Christ. An old symbol of the servant is the oxen waiting for his master's direction: will it be as a dead sacrifice on the altar, or as a living sacrifice pulling the plough?

That is our reasonable response.

## REFLECTION

*What is foolish living? What is reasonable living? How will your reasonable lifestyle show itself today?*

The first century Christian came to Christ, was baptised and immediately became part of a fellowship, a family, a community of God's people. Thus, Paul's first direction in these verses is to show how renewed thinking works out in practice within the new family of the church.

It is a reflection of the individualism of the church in the West that such a community emphasis would be much further down the order of priorities in the curriculum of discipleship today.

The believer is to think 'soberly' (v3), sensibly (as in Mark 5:15), according to the giftedness God has given him. Such gifting is contrary to our deserving (v6). The believer must think humbly of self for he or she is part of a body (v4-5), and therefore is not independent but interdependent.

Paul lists various gifts in verses 6-8 and it is important to note that none of his gift lists, here or in Ephesians 4 or 1 Corinthians 12, are identical. There is a great diversity in God's gifting: it is never static, and God may well gift the same person differently in varied spheres of ministry. The fact that Paul uses participles in describing the gifts shows that they are not to lie dormant but are evidenced as they are used. Paul lists seven giftings here. In the last three he describes the disposition with which they are to be exercised. Note, for example, 'contributing' in verse 8: they are to be generously and rightly motivated, not for self-aggrandizement; taking the lead. They are not to slacken off; but are

to show mercy, a personal intimate service to those in need. They are to do it cheerfully, not in a grudging way.

I recently read an article about the elderly, in which the author said that elderly people are often dominated by a fear of being a nuisance. In showing mercy to the elderly, for example, we must be cheerful, or they may well develop a 'death wish' so as not to be a nuisance any longer.

Here then is renewed thinking in relation to the church: sober, realistic, humble, exercising our gifting in both a joyous and a self-effacing way.

How can you discover your gifting? Ask your church leadership what needs to be done, and ask them to direct you into the area of service for which they believe you are gifted. (Don't add to your burdens the task of discovering your gifts; leave that to your spiritual leadership.) Then get on and exercise your gifts to his glory, within the body of which he has made you a part.

## REFLECTION

*What are gifts for, according to verses 4-5? How can you be more diligent in the exercise of your giftedness? Which of the seven areas of ministry most relate to you, and how can you apply Paul's exhortation?*

In thinking about ourselves in the church we are to be both sober and humble. In thinking about the church itself, 'sincere love' is the attitude which must dominate. Our love must not have any pretence about it: it must be 'fair dinkum'. Neither will it be 'soppy sentimentality', undiscerning in its affirmations. It will cling to and affirm good and disapprove of evil. In the church family, affection and respect for one another are to be the ongoing values.

Paul closes this section with three exhortations. Firstly, all this activity is to be driven spiritually (v11). Secondly, it must never be lacking zeal, 'not being slack', but 'keep the fires of the Spirit burning' (J.B. Phillips). These two are energised by the third, 'waiting like slaves upon the Lord' (Knox translation).

Giving ourselves to Christ's service is both the surest fruit of spiritual fervour and the condition of maintaining the Spirit's fire in us. Zeal and service are inseparable twins. Similarly, if we are to rejoice in our future hope and be patient in present affliction, we are to be consistent in prayer (v12). As service is the feeder for zeal, so prayer is the feeder for joy and persevering patience.

Being busy in our service of others and faithful in prayer are keys to a healthy spiritual disposition.

All this is involved in being 'living sacrifices, holy and pleasing to God' (v1). Such an attitude is eminently practical in our relationships with God's people by being eager to practise, or literally 'persecuting' hospitality – that is, pursuing opportunities to be hospitable with the zeal of the persecutor.

Hospitality, providing haven for the needy, is the key to sharing; prayer is the key to joyous perseverance; and service is the key to spiritual zeal.

According to Romans 1:25, idolatry is the great lie. Worshipping the god of self is the greatest apostasy. The best friend is one who urges us away from self seeking idolatry, reminds us that we are living sacrifices, and that as servants our calling is to serve! When we serve others in the ways outlined in verses 6-8 we are showing in the clearest way our true identity in Christ. This is the reasonable response to God's mercies.

## REFLECTION

*Hospitality was important in the First Century. Why is it still so important today? How does the connection of zeal and service help you understand the dynamics of Christian living?*

The Christian is to resist doing what comes naturally when it comes to responding to antagonism and persecution. Our renewed minds will lead us to bless the persecutor and not curse (v14), to rejoice when the persecutor rejoices and mourn when he mourns (v15). It is natural to do the very opposite.

This section is very much like the teaching of Jesus in the Sermon on the Mount, in Matthew 5:38-48. Antagonism will come to us inevitably because 'the sinful mind is hostile to God' (Romans 8:7). This response is hard enough for Christians to make even without having to deal with the most debilitating situation, that of disharmony in the local fellowship. We all know that such disharmony from the least expected quarter, within the church, can be more draining of our spiritual resources than the antagonism of the world (v16). We need to resist pride, which builds social and intellectual barriers within the church, and to remember that our Lord Jesus is meek and lowly.

Paul continues in verses 17-21, making it clear that a Christian's personal standards are to be of non-retaliation. The believer will always seek to do what is right and seek to do good (v17, 21). It may well be that a Christian in an official position of judge, soldier or policeman will bear the sword of justice, but on a personal level will be commit-ted to non-retribution, thereby leaving room for God's wrath (v19). Vengeance is God's work and he doesn't need our help. In 2 Thessalonians 1:6, Paul makes God's justice clear: 'He will pay trouble to those who trouble you'.

In verse 20, Paul quotes from Proverbs 25:21-22. Does this mean that our loving response is a way of bringing judgement upon the antagonist? It probably means that our response will bring him to recognise his shameful behaviour, and repent. Moffat translates this verse, 'Make him feel a burning sense of shame', and F.F. Bruce comments that our response will 'make him ashamed and lead to his repentance'.[4]

If the believer is committed personally to non-retribution, how will God bring about justice? Most often God will use the authorities and so Paul turns to them in 13:1-7.

## REFLECTION

*Are you facing antagonism because you are a Christian? Pray that God will show you creative ways to respond. How can you overcome evil with good? In a relatively classless modern society, how might we be tempted to show the pride and conceit of verse 16?*

Modern Western societies are very cynical electorates. We often do not think highly of our politics, politicians or government. Paul probably had every reason to share this attitude in Nero's Rome. Yet he says that authorities are established by God (v1), instituted by him (v2), God's servants (v4, 6), and an agent of wrath (v4). Therefore, the believer is to submit to authorities (v1, 5), pay their taxes (v6) and give them appropriate respect (v7).

Paul could have used the word 'obey' instead of submit. By his use of this word we recognise that there is something voluntary and mutual in the relationship: the state has obligations and so do we. Unlike first century Rome, we live in a democracy whereby every three or four years we vote for those who will govern us. Apathy and ignorance of politics can be subtle forms of rebellion against God. We are to vote intelligently, seek truth and make assessments based on biblical conviction, and not simply be swept along by the media. We may choose to write to newspapers, lobby for the good, and even join a political party.

Christians have a variety of attitudes to their governments:

- Ignore them – because we are not of this world or its political system;

- Total adherence to government – because it is regarded as equivalent to God;

- Rebellion – overthrow the government, because it is an agent of evil;

- Limited jurisdiction – to recognise, as does the Lord Jesus in Matthew chapter 22, that the state and God have appropriate claims on us, but that God's authority and claims over us must ultimately take priority.

A word of caution is needed here. By all means, if you believe you can share the gospel by joining a political party, do so; but don't idealise the party. Like religious denominations, all political parties have something commendable about them, but in the end they are all imperfect human groupings. God is a God of order, and the state authority is an instrument of such order. The political party is an instrument of serving human needs, just as the denomination is an instrument of serving the gospel's broadcast. When either a denomination or a political party ceases to do that, and so compromises you by turning you away from doing these things, then it is time to leave – for we have a higher loyalty to God and his purpose than to the organisation.

## REFLECTION

*Compare the motivation of unbelievers and believers in their thinking about submission to authorities. What extra dimension influences the believer in his/her thinking about obeying governments, for example, and the payment of taxes?*

In the late Eighteenth Century, while reading his Greek New Testament, William Wilberforce became a believer. He then read Philip Doddridge's book, The Rise and Progress of Religion in the Soul, and determined that he should retire from being a politician in order to be more directly involved in ministry.

In the case of Wilberforce, friends like John Newton encouraged him to stay on in the House of Commons and to serve the gospel there. He did so, and did more than anyone else to bring about the abolition of the slave trade in 1807. Like the Earl of Shaftesbury who came after him, Wilberforce was a social reformer who worked to establish education for the poor. So many improvements in the fields of health, education, social welfare and public policy, which we take for granted, can be attributed to the work of these Christian politicians of nineteenth century England.

We should pray for more gospel-focused people like this who will seek to serve the gospel's interests with integrity from within our national, regional and local governments. The crucial elements of Wilberforce's spirituality were daily self-examination, prayer, morning and evening devotions, an expectancy of heaven and a recognition of the importance of solitude.

I raise this issue here because, if we are to cope and be fruitful as God-honouring believers in all the circumstances of our busy lives then we must guard and set aside time to think, to renew the mind, and for solitude to reflect on what the gospel says about God, grace, and about ourselves as living sacrifices. Without such solitude, reflection, and renewal, which were so vital to Wilberforce and others, there will not be transformed living and we will be sucked along by the proud, apathetic, cursing, vengeful and cynical world.

How best can you serve the gospel? By being the active lobbyist, or the letter-writer, or the local Member of Parliament?

## REFLECTION

*How important to you is taking time to think and reflect? How can you be more regular in spending time in quiet reflection?*

This section provides one of Paul's more direct references in Romans to the future coming of Christ. His exhortations are built around verses 11 and 12, '...the day is almost here. So let us put aside the deeds of darkness...'

The central motivation for the appeal of verses 8-10 and verses 13-14 is the understanding of the present time: that the day of Christ's appearing is close – the day of 'the redemption of our bodies' (Romans 8:23), the day of judgement.

Therefore, we are to owe no debts but the ongoing indebtedness of loving one another. Just as seeing someone to whom we owe money reminds us of our debt, so too seeing our fellow believers reminds us of our debt of love to them.

In verses 13-14 Paul returns to his 'put off ... put on' language. (See Ephesians 4:20 – 5:2.) We are to put off orgies, drunkenness and debauchery and behave decently (v13). In clear contrast to such godless behaviour we are to 'put on' the Lord Jesus Christ and his righteousness, and not even think about gratifying the sinful nature, that nature which he described in chapters 7 and 8.

Verse 14 is sometimes known as 'St. Augustine's verse'. The great fourth century Christian leader describes his experience[5]:

'I felt that I was still the captive of my sin ... all at once I heard the sing song voice of a child in a nearby house. 'Take it and read, take it and read' ... I stemmed my flood of tears and stood up, telling myself this could only be a divine command to open the book of Scripture and read the first passage on which my eyes should fall ... I seized it and opened it in silence. I read the passage on which my eyes fell: 'not in revelry and drunkenness ... rather arm yourselves with the Lord Jesus Christ; spend no more thought on nature and nature's appetite' ... in an instant ... it was as though the light of confidence flooded into my heart and all the darkness of doubt was dispelled.'

Augustine then relates that when he told his prayerful mother Monica what had happened, 'she was jubilant with triumph and glorified You'.

We must, like Augustine, make sure we get dressed every day – taking off sin and putting on the righteousness of Christ.

## REFLECTION

*Think about what you should take off today, and what clothing yourself with Christ will mean to you. In what way is love the fulfilment of the law?*

Every church fellowship is made up of people from different backgrounds; our unity as Christians is a unity in diversity.

The church in Rome was a good example of such diversity, which if not handled sensitively could become disruptive of Christian unity.

In this church there were believers from Jewish and Gentile backgrounds. The Jewish believers were bound by a law-influenced conscience to observe food regulations (v2) and special days (v5). The Gentiles had no such scruples.

Paul urged each to accept one another, to warmly take each other as companions, just as God had accepted them into his fellowship (v3; cf. 15:17).

Each person is specifically warned in verse 3. The Gentile (the stronger) must not be superior and look down on the tradition-bound Jewish believer (the weaker). Likewise the Jew must not condemn the uninhibited Gentile by slandering him as worldly. Rather, there is to be warm mutual acceptance. Paul calls these issues which have a tendency to divide 'disputable matters' (v1).

What are these matters? First, they are the matters listed here: food (v2), special days (v5) and drink (v21). 'Days' includes Sabbath observation, for if Paul saw the fourth commandment as still binding, he would not have included it here among the 'disputable matters'.

Second, they are those matters on which the Bible does not speak, or speaks about in an open way, so as to allow believers to have differing views and yet still be attached to Christ.

These may include differing views of parenting, schooling, politics, church government, sacraments or music.

We must be careful to recognise disputable matters and not make every issue a gospel issue, or indisputable. Making disputable matters indisputable is easy to do and doesn't require a lot of thought, yet it is disruptive of fellowship and energy sapping to spend time arguing over non-essential matters.

We must also be careful not to turn indisputable matters into disputable ones. The confessing church in Nazi Germany did this when it asked Jewish believers not to attend church, respecting the conscience of the weaker brothers – in this case, non-Jewish believers who were Nazis. Such a request turned an indisputable matter – that all believers, whatever their background, are welcome into the fellowship – into a disputable one.

We must be sure that in the local fellowship we work hard to maintain unity, but at the same time respect our diversity by recognising that we can be different in so many ways and yet still be one in Christ. The foundation of our fellowship is not found in any cultural, political or denominational expression, but in the fact that Christ died and rose for us and that we are in him (v9).

## REFLECTION

*How can you work to maintain unity in your local church and at the same time respect the diversity of those within the fellowship? Is your church known for its warm acceptance of all believers?*

In this section Paul gives the believers in Rome three reasons why they should warmly accept one another and not divide on disputable matters.

First he says, in verse 3, our ongoing acceptance of one another is based on God's once and for all acceptance of us in Christ: 'God has accepted him'.

If God has not made the issue a barrier to fellowship with him, then we must not create more rigid standards than God and make it a barrier to fellowship with us. God accepts us through the gospel, (v4), so we are to accept one another.

Second he says, in verses 5-8, that in the case of disputable matters each person should develop their own convictions. However, verse 6 tells us that those convictions are to be held 'to the Lord'. That is, each person must live before God with their conviction.

So in verses 7-8 we are to live under Christ's lordship; and if even life and death cannot disturb my relationship with Christ then minor matters like food, drink or days should not disturb my relationship to Christ or to his church.

Third, in verses 9-12, who are we to judge one another when it is Christ's own blood which purchased his church? Every knee will bow to Jesus Christ, the Lord, not to you; so stop judging one another. That is the Lord's prerogative alone.

These are good words for us to hear in our diverse Christian communities. It is very easy for us to reduce the number of disputable matters, and then to judge one another over issues that may be no more than a cultural preference.

Paul's ambition stated in 1 Thessalonians 4:11 is relevant here: 'Make it your ambition to lead a quiet life, to mind your own business and to work with your own hands.'

The accuser of our brothers is the devil (Revelation 12:10), and he doesn't need any help from us! The one who will judge us is the Lord Jesus, and he shares that throne with no-one.

## REFLECTION

*What are some of the disputable issues which you are tempted to make indisputable? What are some of the indisputable matters which you may tend to turn into disputable ones? How can you tell the difference between a disputable and an indisputable matter?*

At our sons' school a 'bullying hotline' used to operate. Concerned parents could use the hotline at any time up to midnight. The school took the issue of bullying very seriously.

The apostle Paul takes theological bullying over disputable matters seriously. In verses 1 and 3 he repeats the encouragement to stop passing judgment. The Roman Christians are to make every effort not to cause one another to stumble. Romans 9:33 reminds us that the Jews stumbled at God's way of making people righteous. If people do stumble, we must make sure it is not over disputable matters but only over the indisputable Christ of the gospel.

The basis of all this is Paul's conviction that no food is unclean (v14). Others may disagree, but Paul doesn't wish to argue about this conviction. Rather, the conviction of fellow believers must be respected. Here Paul, as in 1 Corinthians 8:4 and 7ff, is arguing for the sensitive exercise of Christian freedom: love must guide liberty. In other words, we are to be our brothers' keeper. Paul sets forth the following principles.

• Love is to control the exercise of liberty (v15).

• Unbounded freedom leads to stumbling (v13), obstacles, distress (v15), destruction (v21), falling and condemning (v23). This is a serious issue.

• Liberty must be exercised recognising:

the preciousness of brothers and sisters in Christ (v15); the preciousness of gospel freedom (don't act so as to give it a bad name); matters of eating are peripheral (v19-21); life is about building up, not destroying (v20).

• Our convictions about disputables are not for public display (v22).

• The basis of all that Paul says is that the conscience-bound brother does not have an objective case. If he did, then the issue would no longer be a matter of freedom.

To sum up: we are to make sure we don't put obstacles in front of our brothers and sisters in Christ, or destroy their faith by the insensitive exercise of our Christian liberty. The kingdom of God is about righteousness, peace and edification, so we must work for that and keep convictions about peripheral matters to ourselves.

Freedom must be constrained by love.

## REFLECTION

*What are some of the matters that fall into the category of being disputable today? How do you show your respect for both your freedom in living under the gospel, and for other Christians who may differ with you on these matters?*

Paul could easily have concluded his remarks at the end of chapter 14, but he keeps on like a dog with a bone. This is an important issue for the unity and integrity of Christ's church.

Today Christian unity is too expendable. Denominations divide us too easily and even at the local church level we are far too portable. When there is a difference or offence, we tend to just move churches.

Christian unity is God-given. It is precious, and we need to work hard to maintain it.

Paul's word in verses 1-6 is to the strong, the non-Jews. Such people are to take the initiative and bear with those with a tender conscience. In the exercise of freedom they are to build up their neighbour. That's what Jesus did: he did not please himself but bore the burdens of others. The Old Testament, too, is full of examples of perseverance and endurance and of God's faithfulness.

Such consideration in the way we live does not come naturally. We need God's help, and that's why Paul wishes God's blessing on them in verses 5-6.

In verses 7-13 he says that both the strong and the weak are to take the initiative and accept one another.

Jesus again is the model of such acceptance. God doesn't discriminate between the weak (Jews) and the strong (Gentiles). God's church is not exclusive: God's acceptance of both is the basis of our acceptance of one another.

Again, such acceptance does not come easily to us, so Paul wishes them God's blessing in verse 13. In this verse there is a strong emphasis on hope. God is the God of hope; joy and peace in turn cause an overflow of hope. Elsewhere Paul says that the fruit of hope is endurance (1 Thessalonians 1:3).

Maintaining unity will be hard work and we need to keep our eye on the prize. That's what hope does. The prize is heaven – being in the presence of Jesus together with our fellow believers in perfect union.

We need to warmly accept and bear with one another as we live in the light of such hope.

## REFLECTION

*How can the example of Jesus encourage you as you seek to live in unity with believers with whom you may disagree? How might you show that you value Christian unity only lightly? How are you driven by Christian hope today?*

It is not wrong to be ambitious. Ambition is like faith – it is neither wrong nor right. As in the case of faith, it all depends on what you are ambitious for. Ambition for money will make you greedy, ambition for pleasure will make you indulgent, and ambition for recognition will make you self-promoting.

Paul uses the word ambition on three occasions: in 2 Corinthians 5:9, 1 Thessalonians 4:11 and here in Romans 15:20.

This verse is a good reminder that Paul was an incidental theologian and that he was first and foremost a missionary church planter. This does not mean that he was theologically sloppy— the letter to the Romans is testimony to his theological acumen. However, it does mean that all Paul's thinking was to serve the enterprise of taking the gospel where there was no existing church, 'where Christ was not known'. Like Calvin who studied theology in order to be a better pastor, Paul made sure that all truth and insight drove his mission endeavours.

How did Paul view his ministry?

First, all he is and does was based on God's grace (v15), He never forgot his days as a persecutor of the church.

Second, he was a 'minister' of Jesus Christ (v16), a word used to describe serious government service.

Third, his ministry priority (v16) was to pass on to the Gentiles the gospel from God in order that their lives would become an offering acceptable to God (see 2 Corinthians 11:8).

Fourth, his ministry is self-effacing (v17) and it is a result of Christ's accomplishment (v18). Paul is not out to build up a following for himself. His ministry is based on grace, focused on the gospel and undertaken in a self-effacing manner.

Here are some self-evident truths which help us recognise false claims:

• You can't be fit without exercise;

• You can't become wealthy by responding to emails from Nigeria;

• You can't be slim without watching what you eat;

• You can't grow a true church without the gospel of grace being prominent.

Paul is God's instrument to proclaim the gospel to the Gentiles. Where will this lead him? From Jerusalem in the east to Illyricum in the north-west (v19).

## REFLECTION

*What are you ambitious for today? Where are your ambitions leading you? How do your ambitions affect the gospel and its ministry?*

*I have dwelt for years practically alone in Africa. I have been thirty times stricken with fever, three times attacked by lions, and several times by rhinoceri; but let me say to you, I would gladly go through the whole thing again, if I could have the joy of again bringing that word 'Saviour' and flashing it into the darkness that envelopes another tribe in Central Africa.*[6] (Willis R. Hotchkiss)

Ambition such as this, expressed by the apostle in Romans 15:20, will show itself in plans and strategies. Paul's church planting opportunities had been exhausted in the east (v23), so he planned to go west; and Spain was as far west as it was possible to go. Paul would first go to Jerusalem (v25-26) with his collection from the Gentile churches to ease the famine there. The Gentiles were glad to contribute to this (v26), for since they had shared in their spiritual blessing, the gospel, then likewise they should share materially with believers in Jerusalem.

So Paul's plan was for Jerusalem and then Spain, via Rome. Without embarrassment Paul asks them to financially support his trip to Spain (v24). Likewise, missionaries today must never feel self-conscious about asking for support for missionary endeavours. Such requests are actually opportunities for believers to make investments for eternity, ensuring a warm welcome into eternal dwellings (Luke 16:9).

Paul recognised that his plans were in the hands of God and he would come only in the blessing of Christ (v29). Paul further recognised that none of our plans can succeed without the blessing of God, so he urged his brothers to prayer (v30-33).

There is to be no vestige of pride or arrogant self-dependence in our planning or strategising. God is attracted to human weakness and nothing manifests our weakness more than when we call out to God. The Christian life begins with calling on God (Acts 2:21) and so it is to continue, in our calling out to God – for apart from him our plans are meaningless. Nothing so repulses God as human self-sufficiency, pride and arrogance, which show themselves in our prayerlessness – our lack of dependence on God.

## REFLECTION

*How valid is it to make plans for the future? What are their limitations? What does Paul show here about a right attitude, to the financial support of human need and evangelistic missions?*

Paul urges the Romans to literally 'co-agonise' with him in prayer (v30). The word he uses describes a soldier who joins in the defensive line. Such is the nature of prayer: it is seen as part of a battle, a struggle for the gospel.

They are to pray:

• That Paul will be rescued from the belligerent, unbelieving Jews in Jerusalem (v31);

• That the collection among the Gentile churches will be accepted by the Jerusalem church and thus provide a seal of approval on Paul's Gentile ministry;

• That Paul will then be free to come and join them in Rome for further refreshment. He has already referred to this in 1:11-13.

Paul probably wrote Romans during his eighteen month stay in Corinth (see Acts 18:11). Luke's record in Acts, therefore, tells us how these prayers were answered.

The collection was accepted by the Jerusalem church and Paul was delivered from the unbelievers, according to Acts 21. His deliverance came from the unbelieving Roman garrison (Acts 21:30-32), a most unexpected source.

Did he make it to Rome? Yes, but it was not easy. He came via court appearance, storm, shipwreck, snake bite and under chains, as the guest of the Roman government. He had appealed to Caesar and so the Romans brought him, under arrest, to Rome. We cannot be certain whether Paul ever reached Spain, as he hoped.

God hears and answers the prayers of his people, but often in unexpected ways. You may be praying about a matter now; you may be sure that God hears your prayer, and in one way or another will answer you. His answer may well be unexpected, as it was in the case of Paul. Paul follows his benediction about hope, in 15:13, with a further benediction about peace, in 15:33.

Traditionally, letters of the First Century wished for their readers peace and prosperity; Paul changed that in Romans 1:7 to 'grace and peace'. Having made it clear that peace and hope are direct results of God's provision of righteousness in Romans 5:1-2, it is fitting that Paul conclude this section of his letter by focusing on these two qualities. Justification reminds us that God's wrath has been spent and he is at peace with us; and that what God has begun, in giving us a righteous standing, he will complete in our glorification. That is our hope.

## REFLECTION

*How important to your daily life is Christian hope? How important is it to you to know that God is at peace with you? Why?*

At the very beginning of Romans Paul said that the gospel is the means God powerfully uses to bring people to salvation (Romans 1:16). He now lists some of those who have been saved through this powerful gospel. Paul sends greetings to 27 people, some of whom he names; but he mentions more: the church, the household, the brothers, a mother, a sister and the saints.

Some of them are women, some are men. Some have Jewish names like Mary, some have Greek names like Hermes, and some have Roman names like Julia. Some are people of wealth – heads of households, like Aristobulus and Narcissus. Some have an obviously close bond with Paul, like the mother of Rufus, Andronicus and Junias. Some are known to us from elsewhere in the Bible, like Priscilla and Aquila (Acts 18:1-3); others we have not heard of, like Apollos. All their work is elevated and reported to be significant, whether it was teaching like Priscilla and Aquilla, the 'very hard work' of Mary or the hard work of Tryphena and Tryphosa. We don't know exactly what their work was, but it was recognised and affirmed by the apostle.

The description that dominates this section is 'in Christ' and 'in the Lord'. All these people have this in common: they were once outside of Christ; then, when Paul wrote to this church in Rome, they were in Christ. Now, they are all with Christ – in his presence forever, enjoying the fulfilment of their hope.

The world of the First Century was a rough, hard place for believers, but they knew they were part of God's family: knowing God as Father, Christ as their elder brother and one another as brothers and sisters together in one family. Thus Paul urges them to greet each other as siblings 'with a holy kiss' (verse 16).

Paul's words regarding Phoebe in verses 1-2 are significant, as it was most likely she who was the carrier of the letter to the Romans he had just completed. We can thank God for her safe arrival at Rome, her warm reception by the church and the preservation of this first century letter that continues to strengthen the church today.

## REFLECTION

*Look at Paul's descriptions of individual Christians in the list. If he were to include your name in this list of greetings, how do you think he would describe you? What do these verses teach about our unity in Christ, the nature of ministry, Paul's relationship with the church and the power of the gospel?*

In his preface to his translation of the Acts of the Apostles, published in 1955, the translator J.B. Phillips says of the early Christians, '... if they were uncomplicated and naïve by modern standards we have ruefully to admit that they were open on the God-ward side in a way that is almost unknown today'[7].

Being 'open on the God-ward side' could easily describe the believers in first century Rome. There was a refreshing unpretentiousness about the very early church – their self-sacrifice, the quality of their relationships and the depth of their commitment are challenges to us all.

However, there is no such thing on earth as a perfect church, and just as Paul has urged previously in the letter (12:1; 15:30), now he urges them to be on guard against those who seek to disrupt the work by providing teaching contrary to the content of the apostolic gospel (16:17). These are self-serving, smooth talkers looking for naïve people in order to capture them with false teaching. So Paul urges, 'keep away from them' (16:17). It is a simple and stark instruction.

Paul encourages them to be wise and discerning, yet at the same time to be inexperienced in the matter of evil (v19). Such a combination of innocent openness and discerning wisdom is rare. Note that despite everything Paul has taught them about love and respect for one another, that does not mean they can depreciate the truth for the sake of love. Apostolic truth is vital and non-negotiable and must not be watered down so as to be- come all-inclusive. Again Paul refers to the God of peace (v20), especially appropriate here in the context of friction and division due to the work of the flatterers.

However, he assures them, this God of peace will soon end all Satan's activity. Paul (v20) refers back to Genesis 3:15 – 'he will crush your head, and you will strike his heel'. So too, here, God will 'crush Satan under your feet'. The victory over Satan is achieved through the death and resurrection of Jesus but he is further crushed in the personal deliverance of all believers.

As we battle in the midst of this strife, we have the hope of final victory and the presence of God's grace to sustain us in the fight (v20).

## REFLECTION

*How do you continually rehearse the truths of the gospel and guard them against those who would seek to depreciate them? Can you think of situations you have faced where unity and truth conflict? Where do your loyalties lie?*

Paul now concludes this great letter with particular greetings from his close co-worker Timothy (v21). His secretary Tertius, who wrote down the letter at Paul's dictation (v22), sends his own personal greeting; and Paul sends greetings from his host Gaius (v23). Once again we have this glimpse of Paul: not the unapproachable, cold, stiffly orthodox apostle, but the man engaged in warm relationships with the churches. We can't help but be impressed by the warmth of his widespread greetings.

He has offered blessings at 15:13, 15:33 and 16:20 but now he comes to his final benediction which is the longest of all his letters. These are memorable last words - 'to him who is able to establish you in accordance with my gospel, the message I proclaim about Jesus Christ, in keeping with the revelation of the mystery hidden for long ages past, but now revealed and made known through the prophetic writings by the command of the eternal God, so that all the Gentiles might come to the obedience that comes from faith - to the only wise God be glory forever through Jesus Christ!'

Paul ends as he had begun in Romans 1:1-5. There, the emphasis was on the gospel, promised through the prophets, to the effect that the Gentiles might be called to the obedience which comes from faith. Paul never moves far from the gospel. He never forgets his persecuting past, and God's grace in allowing him to come to Christ.

He introduces the gospel, he defines the gospel, he expounds the gospel, he describes how the gospel transforms. Finally, he commits those who have been powerfully saved by the gospel to the God 'who is able to establish you by my gospel' (v25); that is, the apostolic gospel of God's provision of righteousness in Christ, expounded in this letter.

At his final address to the elders at Ephesus (Acts 20:32) Paul showed a similar confidence in God's ability: he appointed elders in each church and 'committed them to the Lord in whom they had put their trust' (Acts 14:23).

God holds, protects and establishes us through the gospel – the gospel which declares those who are in Christ to have an eternally unchanging, righteous status with God.

## REFLECTION

*Write out a prayer to God in response to the truth of Romans. What is 'the obedience which comes from faith' (see Rom 1:5)? What does such an expression teach us about faith?*

In summarising Romans, we return to 'what is possibly the most important single paragraph ever written', in which Paul announced 'something of the grandeur of Christ's saving work'[8].

Think about that: it is more important than a paragraph of Shakespeare, or the economic theory of Marx or Adam Smith, or one of Winston Churchill's famous speeches. 'Possibly the most important single paragraph ever written …'

Paul utilises three words in common use in his day to describe what God has done for us in Christ:

- *Justified* (v24) – a legal term, whereby God the judge declares the guilty to be in the right with him.

- *Redemption* (v24) – a business term. God justifies not on a whim, but on the basis of the work of his Son in laying down his life to buy us back from the bondage of sin.

- *Sacrifice of atonement* (v25) – a religious word. Jesus, by dying, bears in himself the just wrath of God on human sin, so that guilty sinners don't need to bear it.

On the basis of the redeeming, atoning work of Jesus, God declares the guilty sinner to be justified. That is, not only is our sin forgiven, but righteousness is credited to our account. So we stand perfect before God, 'clothed in righteousness divine'.

Jesus Christ is the foundation of our righteousness. Faith, which is God's gift to us – for we have nothing in which to boast (Romans 3:27) – links us to the work of Jesus, our substitute. This truth is the heart of Paul's argument, and the source of our assurance. All religion, the attempt to somehow win and keep God's favour, is ultimately dehumanising – reducing people to nervous wrecks. Can we ever do enough? Religion places on us an impossible burden, and sets us on an unnecessary quest.

Paul's paragraph tells us that righteousness is not only God's requirement, but also his provision. It announces that the Christian faith is non-religious: it is not about what we must do, but about what God has done.

'My hope is built on nothing less than Jesus' blood and righteousness'.

## REFLECTION

*Think about how good, how reassuring, this news is for the uncertain adherents of any religion. Is it not worthy of wider broadcast? How can you be more a part of that?*

# REFERENCES

[1] Article 17, Anglican 39 Articles

[2] Charles Hodge, Commentary on the Epistle to the Romans (Rev. Ed.; Grand Rapids, Michigan: William B. Eerdmans, 1974).

[3] Charles Hodge, Commentary on the Epistle to the Romans (Rev. Ed.; Grand Rapids, Michigan: William B. Eerdmans, 1974).

[4] F.F.Bruce, Romans (Leicester: Inter-Varsity Press, 1983), 230

[5] St. Augustine, The Confessions of St Augustine (London: Hodder & Stoughton, 1992) Book 8, Section 12.

[6] Willis R. Hotchkiss, African Missions in the 19th Century (Sketches from the Dark Continent)

[7] J.B. Phillips, The Young Church in Action: The Acts of the Apostles in Modern English (London: Fontana Books, 1959).

[8] Leon Morris, The Epistle to the Romans (Grand Rapids, Michigan: William B. Eerdmans, 1988) 173.

# MORE IN THIS SERIES

**MARK: The Suffering Servant** *By Jeremy McQuoid*
ISBN: 978-1-906173-55-5

**DANIEL: Far From Home** *By Justin Mote*
ISBN: 978-1-906173-68-5

**1 THESSALONIANS: Living for Jesus** *By Julia Marsden*
ISBN: 978-1-906173-67-8

To place an order call: **0844 879 3243** email: **sales@10ofthose.com**
or order online: **www.10ofthose.com**

a division of **10** of those.com

**10Publishing** is the publishing house of **10ofThose**. It is committed to producing quality Christian resources that are biblical and accessible.

**www.10ofthose.com** is our online retail arm selling thousands of quality books at discounted prices. We also service many church bookstalls and can help your church to set up a bookstall. Single and bulk purchases welcome.

For information contact: **sales@10ofthose.com** or check out our website: **www.10ofthose.com**